I0425878

July 2012

VETERANS PARALYMPICS PROGRAM

Improved Reporting Needed to Ensure Grant Accountability

Accountability ★ Integrity ★ Reliability

GAO-12-703

VETERANS PARALYMPICS PROGRAM

Improved Reporting Needed to Ensure Grant Accountability

Highlights of GAO-12-703, a report to congressional committees

Why GAO Did This Study

The Veterans Benefits Improvement Act of 2008 established VA's Paralympics Program to promote the lifelong health of disabled veterans and members of the Armed Forces through physical activity and sports. Additionally, the act authorized VA to provide a grant to USOC's Paralympics Division, and allowed USOC to enter into subgrant agreements to provide adaptive sports activities to veterans and service members. The act also mandated GAO to report on the VA Paralympics program.

GAO is required to (1) review how VA and its grantee and subgrantees used program funds to provide adaptive sports opportunities to veterans and service members; (2) assess how VA is overseeing its grantee's and subgrantees' use of funds; and (3) describe how veterans and service members have benefited from VA Paralympics activities. To do this, GAO reviewed relevant federal laws, regulations, guidance, agency reports, and a non-probability sample of 21 of 76 subgrant files, consisting of data on about 56 percent of funds subgranted. GAO also conducted site visits to two states and interviewed veterans as well as agency and grantee officials.

What GAO Recommends

GAO recommends that VA take additional actions to improve grantee and subgrantee reporting of expenditures, activities, and participants, as well as USOC's monitoring of subgrantees. In commenting upon a draft of this report, VA agreed with these recommendations and reported that it was taking steps to implement them.

View GAO-12-703. For more information, contact Daniel Bertoni at (202) 512-7215 or bertonid@gao.gov.

What GAO Found

The Department of Veterans Affairs (VA) and the U.S. Olympic Committee (USOC) primarily awarded program funds through subgrants to 65 national and community organizations that support adaptive sports opportunities. However, their respective program expenditure reporting was not consistent with federal internal control standards, making it difficult to know fully how program funds were spent. VA's reporting of first-year program funding was problematic because it did not closely track costs until midway through the fiscal year. During the second fiscal year—2011—VA granted $7.5 million to USOC, which, in turn, awarded $4.4 million to subgrantees and spent the remainder primarily on operations and personnel. Subgrantees reported using funds for activities such as training and camps. GAO found, however, that USOC did not have sufficient reporting requirements in place for subgrantees to provide information on how VA funds were used separate from other sources of funding.

VA relied upon self-reported, unverified information to oversee the grant program but is planning to make improvements. In fiscal year 2011, VA did not conduct any on-site or remote monitoring to verify how funds were used. Thus, VA lacked information on how well USOC and subgrantees managed grant funds, potentially exposing itself to paying for services not delivered. In 12 of 21 subgrant files selected, USOC was not holding subgrantees accountable for meeting the terms of their agreements. For example, one subgrantee agreed to conduct 10 activities, but the file indicated only 4 were conducted. VA reported that it has plans to improve to oversight, including conducting on-site monitoring of grantees' and subgrantees' use of funds and having USOC verify financial reports for at-risk subgrantees, such as those with large subgrants.

While program benefits were reported by subgrantees and participants, up until this point VA has not systematically measured how adaptive sports activities benefit the health and well-being of veterans and service members. Subgrantees primarily report anecdotal information on program benefits, such as individual success stories. VA collects information on the number of activities and participants from USOC. In 2011, over 10,000 participants were served through nearly 2,000 activities. However, these metrics are flawed due to double counting and other measurement issues. VA officials also recognize that the metrics do not comprehensively measure program benefits. Thus, VA and USOC have hired a contractor to conduct a study on the effects of adaptive sports on rehabilitation and reintegration of veterans and service members into the community.

Figures: VA-Funded Archery and Wheelchair Racing Competitions

Source: GAO and U.S. Olympic Committee.

_____ **United States Government Accountability Office**

Contents

Abbreviations

IG	Inspector General
GAO	U.S. Government Accountability Office
OMB	Office of Management and Budget
USOC	United States Olympic Committee
VA	Department of Veterans Affairs

United States Government Accountability Office
Washington, DC 20548

July 26, 2012

The Honorable Patty Murray
Chairman
Committee on Veterans' Affairs
United States Senate

The Honorable Richard Burr
Ranking Member
Committee on Veterans' Affairs
United States Senate

The Honorable Jeff Miller
Chairman
Committee on Veterans' Affairs
House of Representatives

The Honorable Bob Filner
Ranking Member
Committee on Veterans' Affairs
House of Representatives

In 2010, an estimated 3.4 million veterans had a disability due to service-related injuries and illnesses.[1] Due to advances in battlefield medicine, a larger proportion of military personnel are surviving their wounds than in previous generations, though often with serious medical conditions including amputations, traumatic brain injuries, and post traumatic stress disorder. To promote the lifelong health of veterans and servicemembers with disabilities through regular participation in physical activity and sports, as well other related purposes, the Veterans Benefits Improvement Act of 2008[2] established the Office of National Veterans Sports Programs and Special Events within the Department of Veterans Affairs (VA). The act also authorized VA to provide monthly assistance allowances to veterans with disabilities participating in Paralympics competitions or training operated by the United States Olympic Committee (USOC). Additionally, the act authorized grants solely to

---

[1] 2010 American Community Survey data.

[2] Pub. L. No. 110-389, §§ 701-704, 122 Stat. 4145, 4180-85.

USOC[3] to plan, develop, manage, and implement an integrated adaptive sports program[4] for veterans and servicemembers with disabilities, including joint outreach with VA. The act also allows USOC to enter into partnership agreements with other organizations, essentially subgranting funds to conduct adaptive sports activities. VA conducts grant oversight to help ensure that USOC is effectively and efficiently providing adaptive sports opportunities, reliably managing its financial reporting, and is in compliance with applicable laws and regulations. Moreover, the act mandated GAO to submit a report of the VA Paralympics program by September 30, 2012.[5]

In response to our this mandate, our objectives are to (1) review how VA and its grantee and subgrantees used program funds to provide adaptive sports opportunities to veterans and servicemembers; (2) assess how VA is overseeing grantee's and subgrantees' use of funds; and (3) describe how veterans and servicemembers have benefited from VA Paralympics activities.

To address these issues, we analyzed both planned and final program budget expenditure data; reviewed program reports, guidance, and relevant federal laws and regulations; and interviewed VA and USOC officials and other program stakeholders about VA's Paralympics program activities funded with fiscal years 2010, 2011, and 2012 appropriations. Because USOC is delayed by one fiscal year in its use of program funds, we reported their annual budget information separately from VA's annual budget information. We assessed VA's and USOC's budget data and found them sufficiently reliable for our reporting purposes. As part of this analysis, we reviewed subgrantee plans for spending grant funds as reported to USOC. We do not provide information on subgrantees' final, reported expenditures because we found that some subgrantees reported

---

[3]The act actually refers to the United States Paralympics, Inc, but in 2009, when VA was preparing its first grant agreement, it was informed that USOC had dissolved United States Paralympics, Inc. as a separate entity and that it had been superseded by the Paralympic Division of USOC. To ensure grants were used as provided under the law, VA reported that it awarded them directly to USOC.

[4]According to VA, both of the terms "Paralympic" and "adaptive sports" can be used when referring to recreational sports for those with a physical or visual disability. However, "Paralympic" can also refer to elite-level competition. For simplicity, VA uses the term "adaptive sports" when referring to the programs it promotes.

[5]§ 704, 122 Stat. 4185.

spending more than what they were granted, making it unclear to us which portion of their program costs were funded by VA. In addition, we reviewed a non-probability sample of 21 out of the 76 subgrant files maintained by USOC during a site visit to the organization's headquarters in Colorado Springs, Colorado. These subgrant files included information on grant activities that occurred during fiscal year 2011 and were a mix of some that were selected based on their larger size as well as others that were randomly selected. In total, the sample files contained information on 56 percent of funds USOC provided in subgrants using fiscal year 2010 dollars. We also interviewed subgrantees, regional stakeholders, and veteran program participants at a site visit to a VA adaptive sports program event in Chicago, Illinois in August 2011. (See appendix I for more details.)

We conducted this performance audit from June 2011 through July 2012 in accordance with generally accepted government auditing standards. Those standards require that we plan and perform the audit to obtain sufficient, appropriate evidence to provide a reasonable basis for our findings and conclusions based on our audit objectives. We believe that the evidence we obtained provides a reasonable basis for our findings and conclusions based on our audit objectives.

Background

VA's Office of National Veterans Sports Programs and Special Events' mission is to motivate, encourage, and sustain participation and competition in adaptive sports among veterans and members of the Armed Forces with disabilities. This is to be accomplished through collaboration with VA clinical personnel as well as national and community-based adaptive sports programs. This office is responsible for the VA Paralympics program's administration, including the grant award process, grant oversight, distribution of any monthly assistance allowances to eligible athletes, and program outreach. For fiscal years 2010 through 2012, the federal law authorizes appropriations of $2 million for monthly assistance allowances for competitive athletes in training and $8 million for grants to USOC.[6] The grant program will need to be reauthorized to continue in fiscal year 2014. VA officials stated that, in the first years of the Paralympics program—fiscal years 2010 and 2011—$10

---

[6]Sec 702(a), § 521A(g), 122 Stat. 4182-83 (codified at 38 U.S.C. § 521A(g), and 703(a) § 322(d)(4), 122 Stat. 4184 (codified at 38 U.S.C. § 322(d)(4)).

million in federal funds were made available for each year.[7] Prior to receiving this initial funding, the office had a troubled beginning. In February 2010, VA's Inspector General (IG) found that the office's initial director had abused agency resources and obstructed the IG investigation.[8] Since then, VA officials reported that they hired a new office director, restructured the office housing the program, and addressed these issues of malfeasance.

The USOC is a non-profit organization that serves as the National Olympic and Paralympic Committees and, as such, is responsible for training, entering, and funding U.S. teams for the Olympic and Paralympic Games. Furthermore, the organization has a well-established history of providing adaptive sports opportunities to people with disabilities. To reach veterans and servicemembers throughout the United States, USOC subgrants VA funding to national and community organizations that provide adaptive sports opportunities. (See figure 1 for the VA Paralympics program's organizational chart, including external organizations and individuals who receive program funds.)

The categories of subgrantees are:

- National Partners: national organizations that offer camps, clinics and on-going programs for veterans and servicemembers with disabilities through local chapters. Individual annual subgrant amounts range from $100,000 to $500,000.

- Athlete Development subgrant recipients: organizations that conduct a national network of camps and clinics to provide opportunities for veterans and servicemembers with disabilities to receive sport-

---

[7] Although no appropriations were provided under the specific authorizations in the act, the program was funded from VA's Office of Pubic and Intergovernmental Affairs' general operating expenses account. Consolidated Appropriations Act, 2010, Pub. L. No. 111-117, 123 Stat. 3034, 3300 (2009), Department of Defense and Full-Year Continuing Appropriations Act, 2011, Pub. L. No. 112-10, 125 Stat. 38, 174 – 76, and Consolidated Appropriations Act, 2012, Pub. L. No. 112-74, 125 Stat. 786, 1151.

[8] At the time of the investigation, the duties associated with the Paralympics program were being handled by the director of the Office of National Programs and Special Events, which is now a part of the Office of National Veterans Sports Programs and Special Events. For more information about the investigation, see VA Office of Inspector General, *Abuse of Authority, Misuse of Position and Resources, Acceptance of Gratuities, & Interference with an OIG Investigation, National Programs & Special Events* (Washington, D.C.: February 5, 2010).

specific instruction and assessment. These opportunities help participants meet U.S. Paralympics standards of performance for emerging athletes. Individual annual subgrant amounts range from $15,000 to $300,000.

- Model Community Partners: community organizations that provide leadership in various geographic regions for promoting adaptive sports and to help increase regional capacity for Paralympic sports. These organizations are allowed to further subgrant funds to other local organizations to provide direct services. Individual annual subgrant amounts range from $2,500 to $175,000.

- Olympic Opportunity Fund recipients: community organizations that aim to bring adaptive sports opportunities to their local communities. Individual annual subgrant amounts range from $5,000 to $45,000.

Figure 1: VA Paralympics Program's Organization Chart, Including Program Fund Recipients

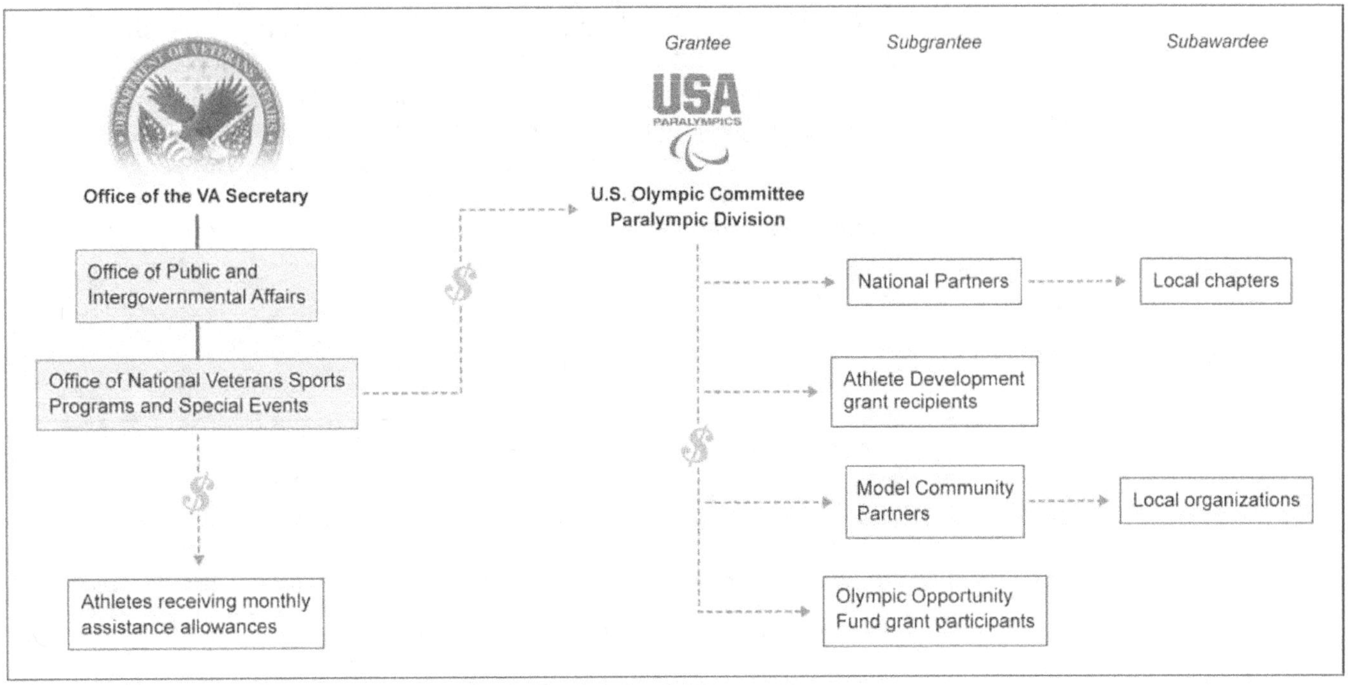

Source: GAO analysis of VA and USOC documents.

GAO-12-703 Veterans Paralympics Program

As a condition of receiving these funds, USOC must permit VA to conduct the oversight VA determines is appropriate.[9] Furthermore, the federal law requires USOC to submit to the Secretary of VA an annual report detailing its use of grant funds. [10] The reports are to include the number of veterans who participated in the adaptive sports program and the administrative expenses. USOC provided this first annual report to VA in November 2011. In turn, VA is required to report annually to Congress on the use of program funds for each year the Secretary makes grants to USOC. [11] Additionally, VA and USOC officials agreed that USOC would submit quarterly progress reports throughout the year. During fiscal year 2011, USOC provided quarterly reports that included descriptions of activities conducted by subgrantees, the number of veterans and servicemembers served in the activities, and anecdotal information on how participants benefited from activities.

Regular reporting of relevant, reliable, and timely information and regular monitoring are necessary for an entity to run and control its operations according to GAO's *Standards for Internal Controls in the Federal Government* and OMB's internal control framework for the federal government.[12] This internal controls guidance states that program managers need both operational and financial data to determine whether they are meeting their strategic and annual performance plans and effectively and efficiently using resources. Monitoring of internal controls should occur within the normal course of business as well as through separate evaluations. Furthermore, members of the Domestic Working

---

[9]Sec. 702(a), § 521A(b) (codified at 38 U.S.C. § 521A(b)).

[10]Sec. 702(a), § 521A(j)(1) (codified at 38 U.S.C. § 521A(j)(1)).

[11]Sec. 702(a), § 521A(k) (codified at 38 U.S.C. § 521A(k)).

[12]Internal controls are defined as an integral component of an organization's management that provides reasonable assurance that the following objectives are being achieved: effectiveness and efficiency of operations, reliability of financial reporting, and compliance with applicable laws and regulations. Internal control, which is synonymous with management control, helps government program managers achieve desired results through effective stewardship of public resources. For more information about GAO and OMB's internal control frameworks, see *Standards for Internal Control in the Federal Government*. GAO/AIMD-00-21.3.1 (Washington, D.C., November 1999) and OMB Circular A-123 Revised.

Group's Grant Accountability Project[13] —a task force of federal, state, and local audit organizations—found that subgrantees, many of which are small organizations, often lack training and experience in grant management. Therefore, the group suggested that government agencies provide guidance to subgrantees on how to conduct financial reporting that complies with federal and state requirements and auditing and accounting standards. The group also suggested that government agencies conduct ongoing monitoring of subrecipients as well as field or desk audits of potentially high-risk subgrantees.

VA Grants and USOC Subgrants Were Awarded Primarily to Provide Adaptive Sports Opportunities, but Reporting on Expenditures Was Problematic

[13]This project was conducted by the Domestic Working Group, which consists of 19 federal, state and local audit organizations and is chaired by the Comptroller General of the United States. The purpose of the group is to identify current and emerging challenges of mutual interest and explore opportunities for greater collaboration within the community of intergovernmental auditors. The group issued a guide for better managing of governmental grants in October 2005.

VA Awarded the Majority of Program Funds to USOC, but VA's Administrative and Personnel Expenditure Reporting Had Weaknesses

In the first 2 years of the Paralympics program, VA granted most of its available funds for the program to USOC, but inconsistent with federal internal controls standards for reporting relevant and reliable information, we found weaknesses in VA's administrative and personnel expenditure reporting. In fiscal year 2010, VA allotted $10 million for the Paralympics program.[14] VA granted $7.5 million to USOC and obligated about $400,000 to contract with a consulting firm to design an outreach strategy for informing eligible participants about the program. It is not clear, however, how much money VA spent, in total, on administrative and personnel costs associated with this program in fiscal year 2010, primarily because VA did not closely track these costs until midway through fiscal year 2011. VA officials told us that the Office of National Veterans Sports Programs and Special Events did not have a full-time program director and was not fully operational until about midway through fiscal year 2011, and as a result, VA did not establish accounting codes for the Paralympics program until that time. VA officials also said that some administrative and personnel costs were charged to other VA programs as general expenses, and therefore cannot be traced back to the Paralympics program. In addition, VA officials said they were unable to obligate the full amount of fiscal year 2010 funds available to athletes' monthly assistance allowances before the end of the fiscal year, due to the delays in establishing the program.

In fiscal year 2011, VA once again allotted $10 million for the Paralympics program. VA obligated a total of about $8.9 million, of which $7.5 million was granted to USOC. The remainder was spent on athletes' monthly assistance allowances as well as agency administrative and personnel costs. (See table 1.)

---

[14]A VA official explained that the Office of National Veterans Sports Programs and Special Events is housed within the Office of Public and Intergovernmental Affairs and included in its overall budget report. VA Paralympics officials stated that, as a result, they assume they will receive $10 million from this total budget each fiscal year. They do not, however, always obligate or spend that much.

Table 1: Fiscal Year 2011 VA Paralympics Program Funding

	Obligated	Expended	Remaining Unobligated Amount
VA Personnel Costs	$11,753	$11,753	$0
VA Administrative Costs	$322,817	$224,285	$98,532
Athletes' Monthly Assistance Allowances	$1,079,000	$675,906	$403,094
USOC Grant	$7,500,000	$7,500,000	$0
Total	**$8,913,570**	**$8,411,944**	**$501,626**

Source: VA Budget Data as of September 30, 2011.

Note: Not all personnel costs for fiscal year 2011 are included in the number above because accounting codes for the program were not established until midway through the year.

VA planned to spend about $1.1 million in 2011 on monthly assistance allowances to assist competitive athletes with their training, but ultimately spent about $675,900. According to VA officials, fewer athletes than expected were able to apply for the allowance, so the Paralympics program returned some portion of the remaining funds to VA's Office of Public and Intergovernmental Affairs general expense account.[15] USOC officials explained that the monthly information an athlete must submit to obtain an allowance, such as a detailed training log, can be burdensome. USOC is working with VA to develop a new online reporting tool to help ease the burden of this monthly reporting requirement in an effort to encourage greater participation.[16]

---

[15]Program data show that the number of athletes who received payment from October 2010 to September 2011 steadily grew from 40 to over 70. On average, these athletes received monthly payments of approximately $700. VA officials noted that the total of $675,906 for fiscal year 2011 included retroactive payments made to athletes in fiscal years 2010 and 2011. And while these retroactive payments are included in the total amount spent, they are not included in the calculation of average monthly payment ($700). In July 2012, following an expansion of allowable Paralympic sports, VA reported that participation increased to 91 athletes.

[16]An athlete's initial application for monthly assistance allowances is partially managed by USOC. Indeed, USOC works with the athlete to submit to VA the necessary paperwork—which includes information on their dependents and signatures from their coaches. The paperwork also demonstrates that the athletes have qualified for Paralympics training camps and competition. USOC also sets the military standards for each Paralympic sport activity. These military standards must be met for veteran athletes to be eligible to receive a monthly stipend.

VA also planned to spend about $334,500 on fiscal year 2011 administrative and personnel costs associated with the Paralympics program, the majority of which was for contracted services. Specifically, within its administrative costs, VA contracted with a consulting firm to provide grants management services, including assistance with developing grant agreements, providing technical assistance, and developing performance measures for grantees. The contractor did not use all of the funding it obligated for this contract, and returned to VA approximately $98,500. According to VA, $11,753 in fiscal year 2011 funds was spent on personnel for the Paralympics program. However, the salaries for the Director of the Paralympics program and other personnel who contributed to establishing the program are not fully reflected in these personnel costs; those salaries were funded through other VA programs because separate accounting codes for the Paralympics program were not established until midway through fiscal year 2011. Indeed, the Director of the Paralympics program was paid out of funds from the Office of National and Special Events. As a result, only those expenses that were incurred after the codes were established were reported on VA's budget for the Paralympics program. In fiscal year 2012, VA's total personnel and administrative costs are projected to increase to about $2.2 million as the fiscal year 2012 budget will now reflect activities and personnel from the Office of National and Special Events, which has been consolidated into the Office of National Veterans Sports Programs and Special Events.[17] Specifically, in addition to the Paralympics activities, the Office of National Veterans Sports Programs and Special Events now funds five additional staff who travel to and administer six separate national events, as well develop related outreach literature for these events.

USOC Used About Half of Its Grant to Provide Adaptive Sports Opportunities

USOC was awarded a 1-year grant of $7.5 million by VA in fiscal year 2010, to be used during fiscal year 2011. USOC was also awarded a 1-year grant of $7.5 million in fiscal year 2011 to be used during fiscal year 2012. In fiscal year 2011, USOC subgranted approximately $4.4 million to organizations to provide adaptive sports opportunities and used the remaining $3.1 million for its operations and personnel and administrative

---

[17]As described earlier, the Office of National Veterans Sports Programs and Special Events is housed within the Office of Public and Intergovernmental Affairs. The old Office of National and Special Events had also been housed within this office.

costs.[18] Some of USOC's subgrantees did not use all of the funding they received for their adaptive sports programs, so they collectively returned about $50,000 to USOC. VA officials reported that USOC returned these remaining funds to VA.

In fiscal year 2011, about half of the $1.5 million USOC spent on operations went towards outreach and awareness efforts as well as program support for the Paralympics sport programs, while the remaining half was used to provide training and technical assistance. For example, USOC works with VA medical centers and local organizations to help them develop relationships and expand opportunities for veterans and servicemembers with disabilities to engage in adaptive sports. USOC's program budget shows that operation costs are projected to decrease to $1.1 million in fiscal year 2012. Fiscal year 2011 was the first year that USOC implemented a VA grant program. USOC officials told us the decrease in 2012 operations costs reflects the fact in fiscal year 2011, there were significant upfront, one-time costs to build the foundation of the program, such as designing outreach materials and regional training. USOC officials also said "lessons learned" from their experiences during that first year will allow them to plan more effectively going forward.

USOC reports personnel costs separately from administrative costs. In fiscal year 2011, USOC spent about $1.3 million on personnel costs. Specifically, this funding went toward salaries, Social Security taxes, Medicare withholdings, and benefits for 17 program staff and additional temporary staff. The salaries of program staff ranged from about $20,000 to $175,000 and covered positions including the administrative assistants, coaches, grant managers, and program director, among others. Further, in addition to having staff who are dedicated to administering the program, USOC has staff dedicated to the outreach and technical assistance efforts described above; they are responsible for designing and implementing USOC's outreach materials and facilitating conferences, regional meetings/trainings, and other training and education activities for veterans.

In fiscal year 2012, USOC projects spending about $1.9 million to pay for the salaries of 12 program staff. As a percent of its budget, USOC's

---

[18]Specifically, USOC's operations costs for fiscal year 2011 were $1.5 million; personnel costs were $1.3 million, and administrative costs were $253,000.

personnel costs are projected to increase from 18 percent in fiscal year 2011 to 26 percent in fiscal year 2012. USOC officials said that the increase is due to its fiscal year 2011 grant with VA spanning a 17 month period of performance. This differs from the first grant USOC received which was for a 12 month period of performance.

In contrast, USOC's allocated administrative costs[19] are projected to decrease from $253,000 in fiscal year 2011 to $0 in fiscal year 2012.[20] Specifically, in fiscal year 2011 these funds went toward indirect costs such as rental expenses, supplies, event expenses, and utilities. A USOC official told us that they chose not to allocate any administrative costs in fiscal year 2012 because they want to allocate the most possible funding to programming that directly serves veterans. USOC reported that it plans to pay for administrative costs associated with the VA program through other funding sources.

Subgrantees Provided a Range of Activities, but Determining Whether They Spent Funds As Planned Was Problematic

Subgrantees reported using funds to provide opportunities in a range of activities—through camps, practice/trainings, and competitions—across 29 adaptive sports. Cycling/handcycling and skiing were the most common activities. (See figure 2.)

---

[19]According to VA General Counsel guidance, the law governing the Paralympics program does not include personnel costs within its definition of administrative costs. For subgrantee use of funds, USOC defines administrative costs to include only costs associated with subawardees and the implementation and tracking of subaward programs.

[20]The federal law allows USOC to use up to 5 percent and subgrantees to use up to 10 percent of grant or subgrant funding, respectively, for administrative expenses (Sec. 702(a), § 521A(d)(4) and (5), 122 Stat. 4182 (codified at 38 U.S.C. § 521a(d)(4) and (5)). At the same time, there are no limits on the proportion of funding that can be used for operations or personnel costs. In fiscal year 2011, USOC's administrative costs represented 3 percent of its total grant amount.

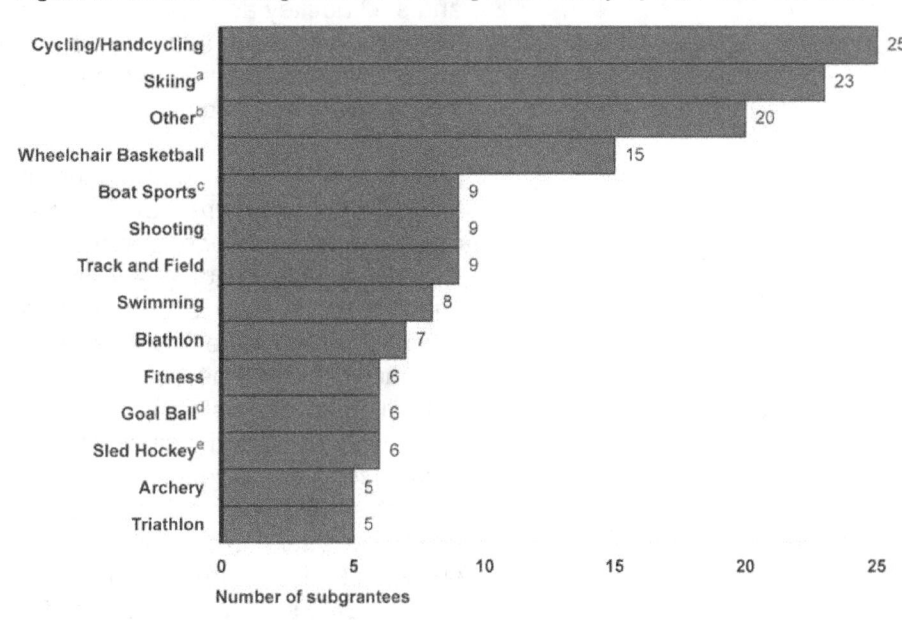

Figure 2: Number of Subgrantees Providing Activities by Sport, Fiscal Year 2011

Number of subgrantees

Source: GAO analysis of sport data in USOC fiscal year 2011 annual report.

[a]The "Skiing" category includes cross country and alpine skiing.

[b]The "Other" category includes bowling, climbing, curling, fencing, judo, powerlifting, road racing, sitting volleyball, snowboarding, surfing, wheelchair racing, wheelchair rugby, and wheelchair tennis.

[c]The "Boat Sports" category includes kayaking, rowing, and sailing.

[d]Goal ball is an indoor game invented for participants with visual impairments in which opposing teams try to roll a ball with bells across the other team's goal line.

[e]Sled hockey is similar to ice hockey in terms of general rules and concepts. It differs in that it allows participants with mobility limitations to sit on an adaptive sled, which is affixed with two skate blades and a runner in the front to form a tripod. The hockey stick has a pick on the end which participants use to propel the sled across the ice.

The majority of USOC's subgrantees received relatively small grants in fiscal year 2011; of the 76 grants USOC awarded to 65 organizations, 54 were Olympic Opportunity Fund subgrants, awarded through a competitive process, ranging from $5,000 to about $45,000.[21] As previously described, Olympic Opportunity Fund subgrants provide adaptive sports to veterans' local communities. For example, one

---

[21]Some subgrantees received more than one type of grant depending on the nature of the adaptive sports programming they planned to offer.

subgrantee reported using Olympic Opportunity funds to provide cycling and sled hockey activities, such as weekly hand cycling clinics and training sessions on adaptive equipment. Another subgrantee reported using Olympic Opportunity funds to hold a weekly power-lifting group, an indoor kayaking clinic, and a judo clinic.

The remaining 22 subgrants generally were larger, ranging from $15,000 to $500,000, and were provided to Athlete Development organizations and National and Model Community Partners. These organizations provided a wider range of activity types through national networks, local chapters, or community organizations in various geographic regions. For example, one Athlete Development subgrantee reported holding an outreach clinic at a nearby VA hospital where they educated staff and potential participants about adaptive sports options and hosted a ski camp which included a sit-ski clinic, a race, and strength and conditioning training for a cross-country skiing marathon. In addition, a National Partner subgrantee reported using its funds to train and educate staff and program leaders on adaptive and Paralympic sports, and to conduct outreach and recruitment campaigns. This organization also awarded and administered subgrants to some of its local chapters to hold archery, cycling, fencing, wheelchair basketball, and swimming activities, among others.

All subgrantees' grant agreements required them to report how VA funds were used to cover program expenses. As part of their agreements, subgrantees provided a projected budget detailing plans to spend program funds in six categories: personnel, operations, equipment, supplies, travel, and administrative costs (see appendix II for USOC's cost definitions for subgrantees' use of funds). Although subgrantees could not spend more than 10 percent of the total amount granted on administrative costs, no other category had spending limits. Of the approximately $4.4 million USOC awarded for fiscal year 2011, subgrantees projected using over half, or about $2.6 million, on operations and personnel costs. Subgrantees projected that these costs would remain about the same for fiscal year 2012. (See figure 3.)

Figure 3: Fiscal Years 2011 and 2012 Projected Budget Estimates for Subgrantees

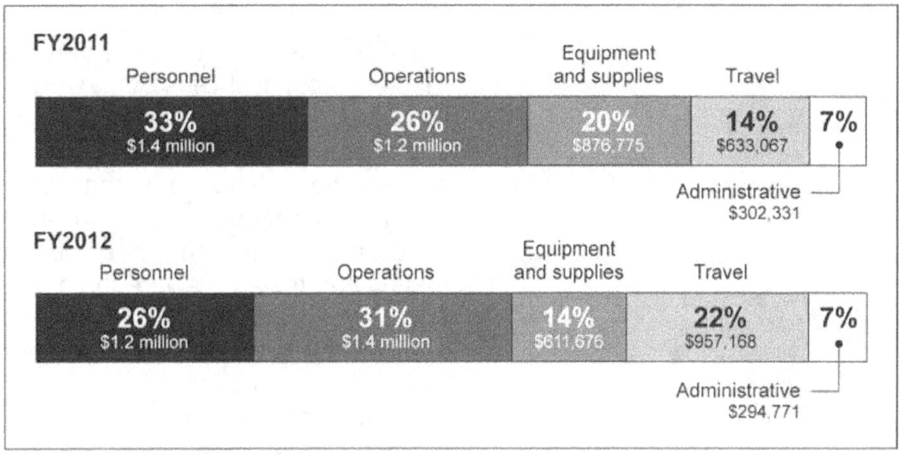

FY2011

Personnel	Operations	Equipment and supplies	Travel	
33% $1.4 million	26% $1.2 million	20% $876,775	14% $633,067	7%

Administrative — $302,331

FY2012

Personnel	Operations	Equipment and supplies	Travel	
26% $1.2 million	31% $1.4 million	14% $611,676	22% $957,168	7%

Administrative — $294,771

Source: GAO analysis of USOC expenditure data

Note: USOC expenditure data reported equipment and supplies as one combined budget item.

Inconsistent with federal internal control standards, we found that during the first program year, USOC did not have reporting requirements or electronic reporting systems in place for subgrantees to provide information on how VA funds were used separate from other sources. As a result, there was a lack of reliable information on actual expenditures. Our review of a sample of subgrantees' files raised concerns with how subgrantees reported their actual expenditures. In 7 of the 21 subgrantees' files we reviewed, it was difficult to determine how the subgrantees spent their grant funding, and 4 out of these 7 files reported spending more than they were actually granted by VA to provide adaptive sports activities. For example, in one case, a subgrantee received a grant for $35,000 but reported expenditures to USOC in excess of $89,000. In reviewing these files, we found that USOC had not determined what portion of the subgrantees' program costs were funded with VA dollars. While USOC provided a template to each subgrantee to report quarterly expenditures, the template did not explicitly request that a subgrantee only provide information on how VA funds were spent. When asked if they reconciled a subgrantee's reported expenditures with planned expenditures, USOC officials told us they generally did not have enough time between the receipt of a subgrantee's quarterly budget and the deadline to submit a quarterly report to VA to ensure that the budget information was accurate. This lack of follow-up is inconsistent with OMB internal controls guidance, which provides that management should regularly reconcile and compare data within the normal course of business.

USOC officials said they were aware of reporting problems and, at the beginning of fiscal year 2012, were developing and implementing an electronic system that will allow subgrantees to report quarterly expenditures online, among other things. USOC officials told us such a system should help them process the reports more quickly. However, they acknowledged the system will not include controls to ensure subgrantees report only those costs specific to the VA grant. VA officials told us that they are aware that this electronic system has limitations and they have directed USOC to make the necessary improvements. In addition, VA reported that it provided guidance on how USOC could improve data processes, and USOC has agreed to send its grant management staff to training, both in effort to enhance USOC's data reporting capabilities.

VA Relied on Self-Reported, Unverified Information to Oversee the Grant Program, but Is Taking Steps to Improve Oversight

VA Lacked Information on How USOC and Subgrantees Used Funds

VA lacked information on how USOC and subgrantees used funds due to its reliance on self-reported, unverified quarterly reports from USOC. Inconsistent with federal internal controls standards, VA officials stated that they did not independently review or verify how grant funds were used due to a lack of staff to oversee the program in fiscal year 2011. In fact, VA did not hire staff dedicated to managing the Paralympics program until it had already granted funds to USOC. Specifically, in September 2010, VA and USOC established a memorandum of agreement for the grant, but a Paralympics program director was not hired until February 2011. The director, with the assistance of interns, reported spending the rest of the fiscal year finalizing the office's outreach campaign, administering the monthly assistance allowance program, and processing USOC's fiscal year 2011 grant application.[22] According to VA officials, another VA Paralympics staff person was hired in September 2011. Furthermore, with the establishment of the Paralympics program, agency officials stated that grant management became a new administrative responsibility for the VA Office of Public and Intergovernmental Affairs as well as USOC and the subgrantees, and all of these program stakeholders needed time to learn about appropriate oversight mechanisms.

USOC officials told us their quarterly reports were primarily based on the quarterly reports they obtained from subgrantees, and therefore, the available information VA had for oversight may not have been accurate. USOC officials managing the grant program did not conduct any separate reviews to verify the information provided to them by subgrantees, and as mentioned earlier, did not make efforts to reconcile expenditure data in these quarterly reports as they were submitted. To gain additional information about how subgrantees were managing funds in the first program year, USOC's Audit Division selected 2 of the 65 subgrantees, based on risk-related criteria, for review in the fall and winter of 2012, and the grant managing officials plan to use the information from those audits to develop future plans for oversight.

Our review of a sample of USOC's files on subgrantees showed that USOC officials were not holding subgrantees accountable for meeting the terms of their subgrant agreements—a grant management problem about which VA was not in the position to know about given its lack of oversight. We found that many subgrantee files lacked information on the status of their grant expenditures and the activities the subgrantees agreed to conduct. USOC reported using a process in which quarterly reports are checked against subgrantees' agreements to ensure completeness of agreed-upon activities. However, in 12 of the 21 subgrant files we reviewed, we did not find evidence that the subgrantees conducted all agreed-upon activities. For example, one National Partner had agreed to develop 27 programs related to handcycling, bowling, and trapshooting, but the reports we found mentioned that only 18 programs had been

---

[22]As previously described, USOC spent program funds a full fiscal year later; therefore, its application for fiscal year 2011 funds was submitted to VA during fiscal year 2011.

completed. Another National Partner agreed to conduct 10 activities related to outreach, introducing adaptive sports at VA clinics, and identifying athletes for higher level of competition, but the case file indicated only 4 of these activities had been completed. Furthermore, in 11 of the 12 files, we did not find any documentation explaining why the planned activities did not occur, nor did we find written permission from USOC to change the scope of agreed-upon activities.

In 5 of the 21 files we reviewed, we found that subgrantees transferred more than 20 percent of funds from one budget category to another without the written permission of USOC, as required by their grant agreements. For 2 of these files, we identified significant issues with the subgrantees' financial management and reporting. Specifically, 1 file belonged to a subgrantee that received a $400,000 grant that was one of the organizations subjected to an audit by USOC's Audit Division. The division officials found that, in addition to making unallowed transfers, the subgrantee had instances of non-compliance with OMB Circular A-122's Cost Principles for Non-Profit Organizations (including unexplained personnel and administrative charges by five employees), did not consistently document and communicate requirements and responsibility related to the VA funds it subgranted to its member chapters, and did not clearly and formally document its methodology for determining and allocating administrative costs to the VA grant.[23] Another subgrantee who made unallowed budget transfers also reported purchasing a van without the written permission of USOC, which is required by the grant agreement prior to making equipment purchases exceeding $5,000. This same subgrantee also received another $35,000 VA-funded grant for which it did not submit required expenditure reports.

VA Plans to Improve Its Grant Monitoring

VA officials recognized that their grant oversight has been limited and report that improvements are under development. In December 2011, VA established a monitoring plan that identifies the specific information USOC should report and requires USOC to establish a similar plan to oversee subgrantees. Specifically, VA's plan requires USOC to submit quarterly reports and an annual report that include summary data on the activities provided, number of veterans served, levels of expended and

---

[23]In its response to the Audit Division, the subgrantee agreed to avoid these problems with future grant funds. This subgrantee received another $400,000 grant from fiscal year 2011 program funds.

unexpended funds, and available assets, among other information. VA's plan does not, however, require on-site or remote evaluations of USOC and the subgrantees, nor a review of USOC's monitoring outcomes for subgrantees. When asked why such monitoring was not included in the plan, VA officials stated that they recognize that a lack of separate evaluations is a gap in their oversight and are working to address this limitation. For example, in fiscal year 2012, VA officials reported conducting on-site visits of USOC to discuss various aspects of grant management. VA plans to conduct additional on-site reviews of USOC and selected subgrantees later in the year.[24] Furthermore, officials are expecting that information from USOC's subgrantee reviews will eventually be incorporated into subgrantee application packages, which they will review before finalizing future grant agreements. Also, after reviewing the first quarter reporting for fiscal year 2011 funds in January 2012, VA officials reported asking USOC officials to provide more information about whether subgrantees were providing deliverables within the agreed-upon timeframes.

With input from VA, USOC finalized a monitoring plan of subgrantees in early 2012 that, in addition to reviewing subgrantee reports, will require USOC officials to audit financial data for subgrantees selected on risk-based criteria. USOC's plan includes a checklist for reviewing and verifying information in these quarterly reports; the checklist mentions comparing the reports to the agreed-upon activities and conducting remote and on-site reviews. USOC aims to conduct enough site visits to review the use of half of all fiscal year 2011 funds. Furthermore, USOC plans to use risk-based criteria to select subgrantees for remote audits of financial data; these criteria will include the size of the subgrant award, additional granting of VA funds to other entities by the subgrantee, and the absence of a current audit report. The remote audits will include reviewing the subgrantees' ledgers and comparing them to what was submitted in the quarterly reports and reviewing documentation that supports selected transactions to ensure that they are compliant with OMB guidance. However, given that we found that USOC was not holding subgrantees accountable—despite having an oversight process in

---

[24]In May 2012, VA officials reported that they are still developing their process for conducting on-site reviews of subgrantees. The officials also mentioned that an internal control expert from VA's Office of Business Oversight has been assigned to advise them on all aspects of the grant process and they expect program changes will happen during the next grant cycle.

place—VA will need to ensure its monitoring efforts include overseeing the implementation of USOC's plans.

Program Benefits Have Been Reported but VA Does Not Systematically Measure Them

Some Participants Have Reported Improvements to Their Health and Well-Being

We found that many subgrantees and participants reported benefits from VA's Paralympics program. Subgrantees primarily reported anecdotal information on program benefits in their quarterly reports to USOC, and USOC then provided some of these examples in their quarterly reports to VA. This anecdotal information included participant success stories, testimonials, and related news articles, and was consistently positive with regards to the program's value in the first year. (See figure 4 for examples.)

Figure 4: Examples of Anecdotal Reports on VA Paralympics Program Benefits

"Kevin is a 21 year old Veteran with a SCI (paraplegia) injury incurred 6/2011. Kelly worked with Kevin on a 1:1 basis for 2 months to train on the hand cycle, eventually leading to him training on his own at home. Kevin signed up for the Marine Corps Marathon prior to his injury. After his injury in 6/2011, Kevin was determined to still compete in this marathon, but due to his injury, he was not able to run, so he wanted to handcycle. Kevin finished the Marine Corp Marathon this past October 2011 at a time of 2:18! It shows that with the right resources, guidance, and determination, nothing can keep someone from attaining their dreams (even if you have to adapt!). Kevin utilized one of the cycles that was purchased through this grant."
– Subgrantee quarterly report

"One athlete stated 'I still find it hard to believe. Me, a C7 quadriplegic, on the water rowing. It feels so good to exercise, and be treated like an athlete. Rowing is a beautiful sport. And now it's my thing.'"
– Subgrantee quarterly report

"An alumni (army sergeant) told us that because of the confidence he gained the first year, he was able to remain sober for the past year (he had been abusing drugs and alcohol and had been arrested several times) and had started college."
– Subgrantee quarterly report

"Benjamin is a Wounded Warrior from Arizona who . . . was no longer affiliated with a military facility, no longer active, suffering from depression and excessive weight gain and coping with a recent spinal cord injury. He came to our Winter Wounded Warriors Camp, Operation High Altitude accompanied by his mom and with a great deal of trepidation. He fell in love with the sport of Nordic skiing and was eager to come back to participate in our upcoming biathlon camp."
– Subgrantee quarterly report

"I have been in a wheelchair for almost 3 years. I have known about the sports that are available and the resources but I only recently took advantage of them. The biggest benefit I have received from going to these events is being around people that 'get you.' I'm not saying that other people can't try to understand what it's like to be in a chair but they will never really know unless they experience it themselves. . . . I've talked to dozens of vets about these events and they all said that these programs have become an integral part of their lives, as well as mine."
– Veteran Participant

"Thank you for the great opportunity, I was starting to feel kind of isolated and this event helped me in so many different ways. It was really good to meet a lot of the other vets and active duty wounded warriors. Thank you thank you thank you, it meant a lot."
– Veteran Participant

"[Skiing] allows you to focus on your abilities rather than your disabilities. You're normal again. You can compete, get your competitive edge." – Veteran Participant, Bi-lateral Leg Amputee

Sources: USOC fiscal year 2011 quarterly and annual program reports and subgrantee fiscal year 2011 grant files submitted to USOC

During our site visit to an adaptive sports event in Chicago, veterans we spoke with also told us how adaptive sports programs have improved their mental and physical health. All six veterans in one group interview agreed that the greatest benefit was to their mental health; they believe that adaptive sports are a tool that helps them deal with depression. They also said that participating in group activities with other veterans with disabilities made them feel less isolated in their challenges. Other veterans said that they had experienced social benefits, including a boost to their self-esteem; one veteran described how he developed long-term friendships during the competitions, and another described how these events show veterans that they can be physically active despite their disabilities. Veterans also told us that competitions motivated them to stay active on an on-going basis and improved their overall physical health. For example, some veterans said regular participation in athletic activities made them physically stronger in their remaining limbs and had improved their balance and dexterity. One veteran in particular told us that he had lost 68 pounds in 4 months due to his regular participation in Paralympic program activities.

GAO-12-703 Veterans Paralympics Program

Counts of Activities and Participants Are Inconsistent, but VA Is Taking Steps to Improve Measurement of Program Benefits

While VA requires USOC and its subgrantees to count the number of adaptive sports activities conducted and the number of participants served, these measurements are not always accurate.[25] In its fiscal year 2011 annual report to VA, USOC stated that over 10,000 veterans and servicemembers participated in nearly 2,000 activities. However, VA officials acknowledged that the participation and activity data are flawed. Indeed, in USOC's quarterly reports to VA, USOC stated there is some double counting of unique veterans/servicemembers and activities due to partnerships and collaboration among the Paralympic community. For example, a veteran might attend activities sponsored by different subgrantees, and each subgrantee might then include that same veteran in their separate count. The extent of this double counting is unknown due to a lack of a systematic review of the activity and participant counts. Although VA is required by law to report annually to Congress on the number of veterans who participated in adaptive sports activities and the administrative expenses, it has yet to do so. [26]

Additionally, in our review of a sample of 21 subgrantee reports, we found some inconsistencies with how subgrantees count program participants and activities, further diminishing the reliability of these data. It was difficult to determine, in fact, how 16 out of the 21 were counting their participants or activities as many organizations had different interpretations of what qualified as a participant or activity. For example, 8 out of the 21 subgrantee reports counted activities that did not have veteran or military participants—some of them even counted purchases of equipment as activities. Also, 6 out of the 21 subgrantees administered more than one type of a VA Paralympics grant and submitted reports where it was difficult to determine which grant corresponded with which counts of activities and participants.

While subgrantees and program participants reported program benefits, VA has not yet systematically measured how adaptive sports activities specifically benefitted the health and well-being of veterans and servicemembers. A couple of USOC's subgrantees conducted surveys

---

[25]The authorizing legislation requires USOC to report on the use of grant funds, including the number of veterans who participated in the adaptive sports program. VA is, in turn, required to report to Congress annually on the use of funds. 38 U.S.C. § 521A(j)(1) and (k), respectively.

[26]In commenting on a draft to this report, VA indicted that it anticipates providing a report to Congress on the Paralympics program for fiscal years 2010-2011 in August 2012.

asking for feedback on specific events or activities, but VA has not conducted a program-wide survey or study to collect information about the various events and their benefits. Absent this measurement, VA largely relies on the anecdotal information supplied by subgrantees and program participants. Moreover, VA officials recognize that participant and activity counts do not comprehensively measure how participation in adaptive sports can improve a person with disabilities' quality of life, including improved physical health, enhanced confidence and self-esteem, reduction in depression and improved relationships with family members and other members of the community.

VA wants to improve its measurement of Paralympics activity benefits. VA and USOC have, in turn, taken the initiative to hire a contractor to conduct a study on the effects of adaptive sports on rehabilitation and reintegration of veterans and servicemembers into the community, including five life domains (self-care, mobility skills, communication with family and friends, participation in society, and acceptance of disability) and the psychosocial outcomes, including self-esteem and quality of life. The study will include a survey of participants in VA adaptive sports activities, with questions focusing on uncovering key life and goal-setting concerns of participants as well as employment and educational goals and opportunities. VA and USOC are expecting the contractor to provide a preliminary report to Model Community Partners by the end of September 2012. They have also planned for the final results of this study to be shared with internal and external audiences, including government agencies, the research community, and the general public. In addition, VA and USOC have tasked the contractor to conduct an assessment of the VA Paralympics program that will include identification of issues, trends, obstacles, and barriers, which will assist USOC and subgrantees with managing expectations and program performance. VA and USOC have required the contractor to provide an annual report on this assessment by November 2012. VA officials told us they have also been assisting the Paralympic Research and Sport Science Consortium with facilitating research in Paralympic and adaptive sports. VA officials stated that this research is focused on activities that would both enhance Paralympic sports and capabilities to provide rehabilitative opportunities to Veterans and members of the Armed Forces with disabilities. In addition, VA officials stated that they are seeking feedback from Paralympic and adaptive sport communities, academia, research institutions, and other entities to try to develop metrics to measure effectiveness.

VA officials stated that the goals of its adaptive sports programming have changed in the past few years with the establishment of the Paralympics program. Prior to the Paralympics program and its current leadership, the Office of Public and Intergovernmental Affairs focused on engaging veterans and servicemembers with disabilities in a few Paralympic sport competitions it sponsored once a year. However, with the Paralympics program and the Office of National Veterans Sports Programs and Special Events in place, VA has expanded its goals to include veteran participation in local and community adaptive sports programs throughout the year and for on-going sports participation to have an impact on the veterans' overall physical and emotional well-being. Further, VA is working with other VA entities to incorporate Paralympic and adaptive sports into rehabilitative whole-life programs for Veterans and members of the Armed Forces with disabilities. For example, VA officials stated that they worked with some of their subgrantees to develop adaptive sports program-related training webinars and other support materials for VA entities such as recreation therapists, centers for blind and visually impaired, and Community Living Centers.

Conclusions

After veterans and servicemembers face life altering disabilities resulting from their service in the Armed Forces, the VA Paralympics program works to empower them to move forward in their next phase of life. In partnership with USOC and its subgrantees, VA has been able to introduce numerous participants to a variety of sports adapted for their physical conditions. Beyond providing access to recreational opportunities, veteran participants told us that adaptive sports have changed the way they think about their disabilities and provided them with opportunities to improve their physical health. As this program matures, it has the potential to provide greater access to adaptive sports and garner a wider range of benefits for participants. VA must, however, improve the program's oversight and reporting to help ensure program funds are efficiently and effectively used. Although USOC is planning various oversight initiatives and is implementing an electronic reporting system for subgrantees, we found that USOC's past efforts at financial accounting, subgrantee oversight, and reporting on participation and activities were weak, resulting in gaps in program knowledge about how program funds were actually spent, whether or not all promised activities occurred, and how many people benefitted from the activities. Moving forward, without this information, VA and policymakers will struggle to make informed decisions about the program's future. VA officials report that they are building a stronger oversight structure, but to the extent USOC's weaknesses remain, VA may miss opportunities to better use program resources to motivate, encourage, and sustain participation and competition in adaptive sports among veterans and servicemembers with disabilities.

Recommendations

To improve oversight within the VA Paralympics grant program, we recommend the Secretary of VA direct the National Director of the Office of National Veterans Sports Programs and Special Events to take the following three actions:

1. Require USOC to modify reporting requirements that will:

   a. Direct subgrantees to only include VA Paralympics program funds in expenditure reports; and

   b. Provide a consistent methodology for how subgrantees should count their program activities and participants, including explicit instruction on what should and should not be counted as an activity or participant.

2. Ensure USOC adds controls to its electronic reporting system that will require subgrantees to identify how VA grant funds were used separate from other funding sources subgrantees use to support adaptive sports activities.

3. Review the implementation of USOC's monitoring plan after a reasonable period to ensure planned efforts were conducted.

Agency Comments and Our Evaluation

VA provided us with comments on a draft of this report, which we have reprinted in appendix III. In its comments, VA agreed with our recommendations and reported that efforts were underway to address each of them. Specifically, VA reported that USOC has already agreed to direct subgrantees to only include information on VA Paralympics program funds in expenditure reports. Furthermore, USOC has agreed to send its grant management staff to training in an effort to improve its data reporting. Regarding USOC's electronic reporting system, VA reported that USOC has included the requirement that subgrantees identify how VA funds were used separately from other funding sources, and VA will review the system before it goes on-line during the fourth quarter of 2012. VA indicated that USOC also plans to provide training to subgrantees on how to appropriately report on grant funds during this quarter. In response to our recommendation on following up on USOC's monitoring plan, VA reported that, in April 2012, it began meeting with USOC to improve USOC's subgrant monitoring program, which now includes weekly conference calls with VA. VA also provided technical comments, which were incorporated into the report as appropriate.

We are sending copies of this report to relevant congressional committees, the Secretary of the Department of Veterans Affairs, the Chief of Paralympics, USOC, and other interested parties. The report will also be available at no charge on the GAO Web site at http://www.gao.gov.

If you or your staffs have any questions about this report, please contact me at (202) 512-7215 or bertonid@gao.gov. Contact points for our Offices of Congressional Relations and Public Affairs may be found on the last page of this report. GAO staff who made key contributions to this report are listed in appendix IV.

Daniel Bertoni
Director, Education, Workforce,
 and Income Security Issues

Appendix I: Objectives, Scope and Methodology

The objectives of this report were to (1) review how VA and its grantee and subgrantees used program funds to provide adaptive sports opportunities to veterans and servicemembers; (2) assess how VA is overseeing grantees' and subgrantees' use of funds; and (3) describe how veterans and servicemembers have benefited from VA Paralympics activities. The mandated requirement to include a description of how the United States Paralympics, Inc. (which was superseded by the Paralympic Division of the United States Olympic Committee (USOC)) used grant funds from the Department of Veterans Affairs (VA) is provided under the first research objective. The other mandated requirements to include the number of veterans with disabilities who benefitted from such grants and how such veterans benefitted were addressed under the third research objective. To address the three objectives, we analyzed both planned and final program budget expenditure data; reviewed program reports, guidance, and relevant federal laws and regulations; and interviewed VA and USOC officials and other program stakeholders about VA's Paralympics program activities funded with fiscal years 2010, 2011, and 2012 appropriations.

Specifically, to determine how VA and its grantees used program funds, we reviewed information on planned and actual program expenditures provided by VA and USOC and interviewed VA and USOC officials to better understand the purposes for which funds were used. VA started spending Paralympic program funds in fiscal year 2010, but did not have complete final expenditure information for that first program year. As a result, we discuss this incomplete expenditure data in our report findings. We obtained VA's complete planned and final expenditure budget information on fiscal year 2011 funds, but could only report planned expenditures for fiscal year 2012, as their actual expenditures for that year had not yet been finalized at the writing of this report. USOC provided data to us on subgrantees' planned and final expenditures. Subgrantees' planned expenditures were based on subgrant agreements made by USOC and the subgrantee, and final expenditures were based on data from quarterly reports submitted by each subgrantee to USOC. To determine the reliability of VA and USOC data on planned and actual program expenditures for that year, we interviewed VA and USOC officials about their procedures for collecting and maintaining these data. In addition, we reviewed a nonprobability sample of 21 subgrant files to verify the accuracy of data reported to USOC and to better understand how USOC maintains these data. The sample included all types of USOC subgrants mentioned in the background of this report. Specifically, all of USOC's National Partner subgrants were included, and if these National Partners were also awarded Olympic Opportunity Fund subgrants, those

subgrants were also included. The sample also included Model
Community Partners and other Olympic Opportunity Fund subgrantees
which were selected randomly after being stratified according to their
subgrant type and USOC-designated geographic region. Due to errors in
the original list of subgrantees by subgrant type provided by USOC, our
sample also included two Athlete Development subgrants. In total, the
sample files contained information on 56 percent of funds USOC provided
in subgrants using fiscal year 2010 dollars. Due to problems we found
with subgrantee reporting, we did not report information on subgrantees'
actual expenditures. (See the body of the report for more information.)
We reported only those expenditure data we believe were sufficiently
reliable for the purposes of our study.

To determine how VA oversaw grantees' use of funds, we interviewed VA
and USOC officials and obtained and reviewed quarterly progress reports
from USOC, examples of progress reports from subgrantees, and VA's
and USOC's monitoring plans. Furthermore, we reviewed the same non-
probability sample of 21 subgrant files to obtain information on whether
their activities were documented as required under USOC policies—
mentioned in subgrant agreements, subgrant applications, and interviews
with the organization's officials—and as promoted by GAO's guidelines
for internal controls and the Domestic Working Group's Grant
Accountability Project's promising practices.

To determine how veterans and servicemembers have benefited from VA
Paralympics program activities, we reviewed participant and activity
counts in the same non-probability sample of 21 subgrantee files
maintained by USOC. We found issues with double-counting of activities
and participants, as well as issues of counting non-
veteran/servicemember activities and participants. However, to be
responsive to our mandate, we provided USOC's total counts of activities
and participants in the report along with a discussion of why these
numbers are not reliable. We reviewed USOC quarterly and annual
program reports to VA. We also interviewed VA and USOC officials as
well as subgrantees, regional stakeholders, and veteran program
participants at a site visit to a VA adaptive sports program event in
Chicago, Illinois in August 2011.

Appendix II: United States Olympic Committee's Cost Definitions for Subgrantees' Use of Funds

Type of Cost	Definition
Administrative	Costs associated with the subawardee and the implementation and tracking of the subaward programs
Equipment	Costs of non-construction related purchases for special purpose equipment that is used for the purposes of the grant
Operations	Includes, but is not limited to, costs of: advertising and public relations related to the federal grant; audit and related services; communication (e.g. telephone, postage); meetings and conferences; participant support; publication and printing; rental of building and equipment; and transportation
Personnel	Includes, but is not limited to, costs of: salaries and wages, director and executive committee membership fees, incentive awards, fringe benefits, pension plans, allowances for off-site pay, incentive pay, location allowances, hardship pay, and cost-of-living differentials
Supplies	Costs of materials, supplies, and fabricated parts necessary to carry out the grant
Travel	Costs of expenses for transportation, lodging, subsistence, and related items incurred by employees in travel status on official business

Source: US Olympic Committee

Appendix III: Comments from the Department of Veterans Affairs

DEPARTMENT OF VETERANS AFFAIRS
Washington DC 20420

July 10, 2012

Mr. Daniel Bertoni
Director, Education, Workforce,
 and Income Security Issues
U.S. Government Accountability Office
441 G Street, NW
Washington, DC 20548

Dear Mr. Bertoni:

The Department of Veterans Affairs (VA) has reviewed the Government Accountability Office's (GAO) draft report, *"VETERANS PARALYMPICS PROGRAM: Improved Reporting Needed to Ensure Grant Accountability"* (GAO-12-703) and concurs with GAO's findings.

The enclosure specifically addresses GAO's recommendations, provides an action plan, and provides technical comments. VA appreciates the opportunity to comment on your draft report.

Sincerely,

John R. Gingrich
Chief of Staff

Enclosure

Enclosure

Department of Veterans Affairs (VA) Comments to
Government Accountability Office (GAO) Draft Report
"VETERANS PARALYMPICS PROGRAM:
Improved Reporting Needed to Ensure Grant Accountability"
(GAO-12-703)

GAO Recommendation: To improve oversight within the VA Paralympics grant
program, the Secretary of VA should direct the National Director of the Office of
National Veterans Sports Programs and Special Events to:

Recommendation 1: Require USOC to modify reporting requirements that will:

    a. Direct subgrantees to only include VA Paralympics program funds in
       expenditure reports;
    b. Provide a consistent methodology for how subgrantees should count their
       program activities and participants, including explicit instruction on what
       should and should not be counted as an activity or participant.

VA Comment: Concur. VA has developed a grant monitoring plan and provided it to
the USOC that specifically addresses oversight of grant funds. The USOC is following
the methodology outlined in VA's grant monitoring plan and will incorporate it in
subsequent reports. VA and the USOC have already implemented elements of the plan
that will be reflected in the USOC's upcoming 3rd quarter reports to VA. VA has asked,
and USOC has agreed, to direct subgrantees to only include VA Paralympic program
funds as specified in the recommendation. VA and USOC are working with
subgrantees to implement these new requirements in any future grant applications.

Additionally, VA personnel attended grant training, and USOC agreed to send their
grant management personnel to the same training curriculum provided to VA grant
managers.

Recommendation 2: Ensure USOC adds controls to its electronic reporting system
that will require subgrantees to identify how VA grant funds were used separate from
other funding sources subgrantees use to support adaptive sports activities.

VA Comment: Concur. At the request of VA, the USOC has developed the tool to
accomplish this recommendation. The new tool will provide an electronic reporting
system that will require subgrantees to identify how VA grant funds were used
separately from other funding sources to support adaptive sports activities. VA will
review the USOC system before it goes online to ensure that it meets VA needs. The
system is expected to be operational in the fourth quarter of 2012. The USOC will also
provide training in the fourth quarter of 2012 to subgrantees on appropriate reporting.

VA Recommended Change: VA additionally recommends revising Recommendation
2 to read as follows: *"Ensure USOC adds controls to its electronic reporting system that*

1

Enclosure

Department of Veterans Affairs (VA) Comments to
Government Accountability Office (GAO) Draft Report
"VETERANS PARALYMPICS PROGRAM:
Improved Reporting Needed to Ensure Grant Accountability"
(GAO-12-703)

will require subgrantees to identify how VA grant funds were used separately from other funding sources subgrantees use to support adaptive sports activities."

Recommendation 3: Review the implementation of USOC's monitoring plan after a reasonable period to ensure planned efforts are conducted.

VA Comment: Concur. Beginning in April 2012, VA and USOC staff began developing an enhanced grant monitoring program. VA and USOC staff met in June 2012 to finalize and approve an enhanced USOC grant monitoring program, and will meet quarterly to review and continue progress. In June, the USOC reorganized staff to put full-time emphasis on grant oversight and monitoring and beginning in July, VA and USOC began conducting weekly grant oversight conference calls to review subgrantee status.

2

Appendix IV: GAO Contact and Staff Acknowledgments

GAO Contact	Daniel Bertoni, 202-512-7215, or bertonid@gao.gov
Staff Acknowledgments	In addition to the contact named above, the following staff members made important contributions to this report: Brett Fallavollita, Assistant Director; Danielle Giese, Analyst-in-Charge; Kristy Kennedy; Nisha Hazra; and Juliann Gorse. Also, Shana Wallace provided guidance on the study's methodology; Craig Winslow provided legal advice; James Bennett assisted with report graphics; and Susannah Compton provided writing assistance.

Related GAO Products

VA Mental Health: Number of Veterans Receiving Care, Barriers Faced, and Efforts to Increase Access. GAO-12-12. Washington, D.C.: October 14, 2011.

VA Education Benefits: Actions Taken, but Outreach and Oversight Could Be Improved. GAO-11-256. Washington, D.C.: February 28, 2011.

VA Health Care: Spending for and Provision of Prosthetic Items. GAO-10-935. Washington, D.C.: September 30, 2010.

Standards for Internal Control in the Federal Government. GAO/AIMD-00-21.3.1 Washington, D.C.: November 1, 1999.

GAO's Mission	The Government Accountability Office, the audit, evaluation, and investigative arm of Congress, exists to support Congress in meeting its constitutional responsibilities and to help improve the performance and accountability of the federal government for the American people. GAO examines the use of public funds; evaluates federal programs and policies; and provides analyses, recommendations, and other assistance to help Congress make informed oversight, policy, and funding decisions. GAO's commitment to good government is reflected in its core values of accountability, integrity, and reliability.
Obtaining Copies of GAO Reports and Testimony	The fastest and easiest way to obtain copies of GAO documents at no cost is through GAO's website (www.gao.gov). Each weekday afternoon, GAO posts on its website newly released reports, testimony, and correspondence. To have GAO e-mail you a list of newly posted products, go to www.gao.gov and select "E-mail Updates."
Order by Phone	The price of each GAO publication reflects GAO's actual cost of production and distribution and depends on the number of pages in the publication and whether the publication is printed in color or black and white. Pricing and ordering information is posted on GAO's website, http://www.gao.gov/ordering.htm. Place orders by calling (202) 512-6000, toll free (866) 801-7077, or TDD (202) 512-2537. Orders may be paid for using American Express, Discover Card, MasterCard, Visa, check, or money order. Call for additional information.
Connect with GAO	Connect with GAO on Facebook, Flickr, Twitter, and YouTube. Subscribe to our RSS Feeds or E-mail Updates. Listen to our Podcasts. Visit GAO on the web at www.gao.gov.
To Report Fraud, Waste, and Abuse in Federal Programs	Contact: Website: www.gao.gov/fraudnet/fraudnet.htm E-mail: fraudnet@gao.gov Automated answering system: (800) 424-5454 or (202) 512-7470
Congressional Relations	Katherine Siggerud, Managing Director, siggerudk@gao.gov, (202) 512-4400, U.S. Government Accountability Office, 441 G Street NW, Room 7125, Washington, DC 20548
Public Affairs	Chuck Young, Managing Director, youngc1@gao.gov, (202) 512-4800 U.S. Government Accountability Office, 441 G Street NW, Room 7149 Washington, DC 20548

www.ingramcontent.com/pod-product-compliance
Lightning Source LLC
Chambersburg PA
CBHW080932290526
45795CB00007BA/2726